RANSOM

T0332760

BY THE SAME AUTHOR

POETRY

Soft Keys
Raising Sparks
Burning Babylon
Corpus
The Half Healed
Drysalter
Selected Poems
Mancunia

FICTION

Patrick's Alphabet
Breath

NON-FICTION

Edgelands (*with Paul Farley*)
Deaths of the Poets (*with Paul Farley*)

RANSOM

Michael Symmons Roberts

CAPE POETRY

1 3 5 7 9 10 8 6 4 2

Jonathan Cape, an imprint of Vintage, is part of the Penguin Random House group of companies whose addresses can be found at global.penguinrandomhouse.com.

Penguin
Random House
UK

Copyright © Michael Symmons Roberts 2021

Michael Symmons Roberts has asserted his right to be identified as the author of this Work in accordance with the Copyright, Designs and Patents Act 1988

First published by Jonathan Cape in 2021

penguin.co.uk/vintage

A CIP catalogue record for this book
is available from the British Library

ISBN 9781787333123

Typeset in 11/13 pt Bembo by Jouve (UK), Milton Keynes

Printed and bound in Great Britain by TJ Books Limited, Padstow, Cornwall

The authorized representative in the EEA is Penguin Random House Ireland,
Morrison Chambers, 32 Nassau Street, Dublin D02 YH68

Penguin Random House is committed to a sustainable future
for our business, our readers and our planet. This book is made
from Forest Stewardship Council® certified paper.

for my sister Deborah

A man will be imprisoned in a room with a door that's unlocked and opens inwards; as long as it does not occur to him to pull rather than push.

Ludwig Wittgenstein

CONTENTS

III

I

THE NOTE

I had in mind your captor
at a hotel desk with an inverse view

(no ocean vista, just bins
and air-con viscera)

tongue out to concentrate,
scissors and glue,

a stack of newspapers
to spell out where and when,

the cost of your release.
Instead, when it came

the note was the start of a song,
single and sustained,

so I put it on repeat,
as I walked, drove, worked, ate,

trying to tease out bird-calls,
timbre of passing cars,

dialects of distant dogs,
to figure where they held you.

When you walked in,
you scared the life out of me.

THE TEARS OF THINGS

Security cameras are singing tonight
out across still streets,

hypermarket car parks,
driveways like jetties

with their harboured,
spotlit family saloons,

the night sky winter-clear,
universe bent to the shape of an eye,

curved to the full extent of vigilance.
To mark out such a clean line

between safe and unsafe, good and wicked,
is to give each solid ground,

a sense of what it's not.
But now, viewed on a phone,

the ultra-foreground is alive with rain,
lit by a meteor shower,

a hail of silver bullets,
lacrimae rerum on the wrong side of the lens.

If the things of the world are crying
it cannot be to honour us,

but dispassionate, and for themselves.
My neighbour leaves home and walks out of shot,

his progress handed from camera
to camera until the land runs out.

The tears of things,
not salt, but rips,

the world an old cloth map of itself,
moth-holed, inks still bold,

but stitches blown
and blanks showing through all over.

WARE

If it helps,
think of this malicious code
as pondweed,
torsion tuned to panic;
holds you closer every time you kick,

but will release you
in the nick; as long as all is paid
your lungs are yours again.

Or think of caution,
watchful, lamps kept lit,
spring spent mending fences,
eyes on winter
and the warning cry of *freeze*.

Think of your data
not as seized, but read and understood
so deeply that your goods

and ours are one,
as trees beneath the forest floor
tend to their weak,
roots as vascular utopia,
our lock on you no jail-cell

but a curl of hair
shut in a heart-shaped pendant.

SONG FOR A SIGN-WALKER

Life and love are all about water
or so says the top line of a placard
hand-painted by a rough sleeper whose path
I cross twice in the same afternoon.
There's a screed of text below,
but no one reads beyond his opening salvo.

He's trying to catch my eye so I keep
my head down, stare at my shoes,
guided by flagstones, road markings, hunch.
His line's not wrong, save by omission,
I tell myself the last words of his sign
will be *unconditional love* not *endless fire.*

When I look up, we're decades on —
crazy fashions, car-less roads, skyscrapers
slim as lift-shafts — but our faces are as was,
mask and giveaway, same cares and passions.
Rivers have risen to meet us.
Forgive me if I have misunderstood.

SKELMERDINE NURSERIES

Must have driven down this road ten thousand times
and never stopped.
Cut-through between peaks and city outskirts,
flat and ever semi-flooded.

Some hacker has seized all our memories,
demanded release-fees none of us can pay,
so in the absence of our portals
all we have is local, real.

Forcing-houses with their rows of fir and spruce
in a headlong race for Christmas,
held in a thick, sweet miasma of themselves,
nurtured *in vitro*.

First day of advent each year
the owner parks his retro camper-van beside
the polytunnels and he sleeps
with a baseball bat to hand,

although the police have said:
To steal large quantities of Christmas trees
is very hard to do.
At least the radio is still on speaking terms

and the rules of engagement are clear enough
– grow then cut, grow then cut –
and in between comes beauty,
on which all depends.

Must have known this whole escapade was being
nurtured under glass,
such simplicity, such flourishing,
spruce, fir, pine in sub-soil polyphony

and the ancestral spirits of the plain
smoke at night in the pre-assembled summerhouses,
in memory of their breath.
Must have taken this short-cut so many years

that I forget to nod
to the nurseries' landmark statue of an armless
Venus, decapitated, tilted to the road like
a ship's figurehead. I never stop.

HELD TO

No matter how early I woke up
there was a bowl of figs, dates, damsons
from the lavish gardens, a bag
of butcher's cuts alongside:
a cherry of blood in its toe.
All lawns cut, watered,
roses dead-headed.

The three-legged mastiff, silent, ancient –
don't touch him, he is here for your protection –
sleeps long days in the shade-grid of his cage.

I don't know how the gates work.
There's a buzz I mistake for a wasp
whenever the cameras tilt
their gargoyle-faces to follow a tic.
Otherwise too quiet, just
a lizard held by its own voltage
halfway up a wall of flaking heaven-blue,
kitchen with its slow tornado of houseflies.

The old set just plays DVDs,
a trilogy, *Godfather 1, 2, 3*, is all.
I know the scripts off-pat.
One night, in storms,
as the bodies were hanging
out of shot-up cars,
the picture scrambled into shash
and a figure danced through it –
a love song in a blizzard,
fugitive signal briefly caught –
then it cut back to the scene
with a horse-head in the bed.

Doors, French windows, all unlocked.
What is the transaction here?
One evening I walked up to the master gate,
pushed and it opened.
So I pulled it shut again.
Later that night I heard distant music,
celebrations of a kind.
I am trying to piece it all together
from the decor, pictures, books they keep.
The flies are driving me insane.

ANOTHER WORD FOR HEART-SHAPED

No rare compass, just a pump,
a balled and unballed fist,
an ache, zero-sum rhythm,
a sump of half-remembered tenderness,

some hook-up to a signal
that keeps dropping out, then flickering on,
a beacon on a distant hill,
sputtering, then flaring strong.

The word *cordate* a promissory note,
home to the machine's true ghost,
a word that catches in your throat,
a sign-up to be won, torn, lost.

PAEAN FOR A BARFLY

You beauty, unlearnt lesson,
you something understood
and then scrambled, you static-charged,
never still for long enough
to swat or to admire,
high-lifer in drab garb,
harbinger of sickness, networker,
joiner-up of haute cuisine and dog-shit,
dancer to muzak,
chancer with your back to the ceiling,
answer to a poor germ's prayers,
you drive us spare,
buzz as you brush past an ear,
licker of lipstick off sweet rims of glasses,
kicker of salt-grains off bar-snack mountains,
ligger, jigger, back-boiler winterer,
semblance of monster,
megalomaniac hobbled by scale,
bouncer off blue lights
bloodsucker after drunken fights,
alighter on optics,
player of bottles as xylophones,
spirit-toper, spray-dodger,
sworn-at swarm of one,
contraption so wonderfully made,
leg-tongued sprung trap,
monochrome hummingbird,
one-word liturgy,
fruit-splitter, sugar-spitter, old red-eyes,
denizen of lock-ins,
egg-layer, soothsayer,
destined to serve the world of this bar,
thankless, rank-less holy star.

BEHEADING THE HORSE

Once the last of the sawing is done,
bone uncoupled from bone
neck's latch lifted from its shoulders
as if to leave a centaur

half-built on the cold-stone flags,
I light up, take a drag,
turn my back on the cobalt eye
that gawps up from the floor at me.

I wrap the head in my old trenchcoat,
lay it on the passenger seat,
then strike out down unlit back roads,
to the motorway. It's good,

I tell myself, to find such a perfect head
for the job. That being said,
it makes a disconcerting fellow traveller
and this odyssey will take me hours.

Fog-lights on. My nerves are shot.
The radio keeps cutting out
so nothing in my car can drown
this awkward, shifty one-to-one.

I swear I keep seeing it flinch
every time I clear my throat,
or retch. I'm gagging on its stench
as it bleeds on my beige bucket-seat.

Then the coat slips off: one naked
eye stares up from the sheer
Vantablack chasm of this head,
as if someone cut a tan leather

horse-face mask, leaving me this horror.
I'm lost in the middle of nowhere,
when, no lie, this beast begins to talk.
I'd like to say its homily was hindmilk,

that it led me into some repentance.
In truth it was just nonsense.

MY WINDOW BECOMES A
JOSEPH CORNELL SHADOW BOX

Days contracted to a span,
so the crab-apple crown
outside this upstairs room
becomes a framed universe
where each morning goldfinches
– thorn-eaters, four or five –
twitch on unseen strings.

In afternoon's slow fade
the frame fills up with votives:
flamingo's leg, wax toad,
an amateur painter's *pietà*,
a newspaper photo of Vesna Vulović –
flight attendant and survivor
of the highest-ever fall.

But I miss those *cardellinos*,
hope that if enough attention
is paid to their absence,
it will render them present,
perched on a toad's back,
cupped in the baby's open hands,
real but unstable here.

EPISODICS

i.m. DSR

(i)

I am allowed upstairs into the
room one final time before
as a morning deluge
on your window
forms a rood screen
to keep outside from in
but not enough

(ii)

not you
this is not your face
sudden tipped
against the wing of your chair
as if in sleep
on the windowsill a joke-
book half-read
TV powered down
so because you always
kissed me on top of my head
I kiss the top of this now
not your true brow
but as present
as your missing from

(iii)

our world uncompassed
turns on this one chair
a spindle
none of us
our whole
your sleepless nightwatch

(iv)

these words cannot hold
or conjure you
I felt I should take
a photograph one last of you
since we would never
be in the same room again
but then knew
I should not

(v)

November glory
rain to snow to
ice-clear hours cut quick
hidden details
rendered visible
this is the first day
in eight decades that has not held
you in its palm I wished so
much that you were of
in

nineteen months on
seventy-six messages still
on voicemail because
I know the first one is
from you and cannot
work my way back along a
rosary of pointless calls
I can only wait
neither listen nor delete
until our house is empty
play it to the walls
your voice so loved
now feared
for what its sounding out
might do to us
record it let it tell us
there's no urgency
it's nothing
you will call us back anon
and none
of this is done or will get done

(vii)

June
a bead curtain at the back door
keeps flies out
photographs
home movies
I have looked and
none of them still
holds you in it
your sudden vanishing
has emptied them
left us with facsimiles
but still we have your voice
in amber

(viii)

what to do
about this play-out
you and not you there
un-listened-to yet somehow heard
that day I gave you all
the words you gave to me
of love of thankfulness
then kissed your grey–
black stripe of hair
and knew you were
will be not there

(ix)

your remark once
that when
you reached the next place met
your dad in his good black suit
your mum stooped in her
green glass beads
then your ancestors
welcoming along the row
until they spoke
a tongue you didn't know
you would embrace
you are not caught
by this
not here
this fallen elegy
that misses every mark

(x)

a blue paisley bathrobe
in your fitfulness
you used to doze
in front of rolling news
screen now blanked
your head
bowed on a tilt not cold
not wax the same warmth
as this room the morning in it
now rude sun
chance gone to say the things
I'm sure you know
I mean
not least of gratitude

(xi)

I hear you say again and again
as once you told me
inside I am
always twenty-one
all continuity
you held together by
on-being and ongoing
now breaking
into episodes
a cut thread so glass beads
roll out across the floor

(xii)

at night I hear them
scatter to the edges
of each room
in search of cracks knot-holes
gaps under skirting-boards
they drop
to the next floor down
and roll
then fall to floors
this house does not possess
another and another
night on night
looking for true ground

(xiii)

three years on
the message light
still blinks
this is what outside contains
mud like slip and hillside sinks
water rattles through the drains
under scrub trees
hawthorn elder
lies a badger's rotten pelt
alive with

(xiv)

There is nothing I can tell you

ON MATTER

A bell about to go,
and the whole class waits for it,

cut off by glass from a film
of summer: pollen-electric, hazy;

distant moped, uncut grass,
spilt oil and tacky pavements.

Too hot for energy transfer,
atoms busy being ordinary. *Questions?*

So the youngest child asks
What if there was none of it?

(no dirt-tracks, palaces, oranges,
no painted dogs, rip-tides, no trees)

and the answer comes back *Nothing,
it's simple, go, so I did.* Back,

a slipstream of colours,
months and years unravelling,

a glove pulled inside-out,
blink-and-you-miss-them millennia,

the wrong side of *ex nihilo*,
a place the incarnate cannot reach,

inverse starburst, reclaimed sigh,
the inside of a buried box,

beats between words, lost for,
absence of absence,

fantastic isotopes,
a telescope turned upside down,

and maybe some clues,
partial previews, flash-frames,

a stranger's half-formed face;
how stuff looked before it was;

next season's growth on the may;
a curved ball with no ball.

No matter, because this rabbit-hole
of dark unmattering has nothing

at the end of it, no being
or not being anti, nobody to care.

II
VINGT REGARDS

1. INTERVIEW WITH OLD PARTISAN IN PARISIAN BAR, 1944

I long for nothing but to hold him close.
Well, I long for liberation and a madeleine.
To see my own son out of uniform. Cigars.

Another coffee? No, my heart's all skitters as it is.
A long, slow cigarette may serve me better,
as the smoke may help me hide these tears.

I've let my mask slip more as I've got older,
learned to tell my loves, tried to forgive.
I'll never speak to occupying soldiers.

Is that it? I pity my poor pulse still stamping out
the seconds for these withered hands.
But the waiting I must do, it has no limit.

I know the *nunc dimittis* to the letter,
but I will not sing until he's in my arms,
my God, my hope, conspirator, creator.

When I say hold, I mean like *this*.
When I say close, you know I mean *this* close.
I will remember you in my prayers.

The dancers are stretching, loosening
in their dressing rooms, half made-up

in a mess of costume rails, water-glasses
topped with a dusting of rouge.

Although it's still too soon to dance,
look at the rush of guttered rain through grids

to join the surge towards an open sea.
See how the dry leaves catch in corners,

petals of a burnt manifesto
caught in a breeze between tenements.

And after curfew watch our flags
lift in unison like unbowed heads to mock us,

because the dance, though fugitive, is here,
and will not be held back.

Already it breaks on the roofs of our mouths
and we can barely contain the taste.

It is there in the off-key buskers, dog-howls,
click of the heels of those uniformed men

who think they hold this city captive still,
and soon must think again.

3. BY WHOM EVERYTHING WAS MADE

It is the set designer's curse,
to lose all trust in what appears,
never off guard in case that door
you thought would open onto boulevards,
or bedrooms turns to balsa in your hand,

swings open to reveal the wooden struts
that prop up the façade,
or in a restaurant you notice
that the drapes are not hemmed,
stale bread, apple juice for brandy.

It must stoke in you a rage for truth,
to tear down flats and props,
gut the canvas, shatter all the sugar-glass,
ask questions that could only be answered
by your truest lovers, oldest friends.

Then set light to what remains,
until you kneel on blackened ground,
bury your face and eat the dirt.

4. SCENE BEFORE THE ANNUNCIATION

Was it the bells across the city
that woke me, or the fact that you are perfect –
my nose in the nape of your neck?
A blue flake falls from the ceiling
onto your pillow and melts:
rare variant of snow, a cut-out shape
uncoupled from its complement,
rehearsal for a time when this house
is in ruins and the wet will claim it.

Or rather a reminder of the strength it takes
to hold back all eternity,
how we are shielded from it
but its sheer weight sometimes
shakes the painted firmament.
A voice calls in the street below a name
that could be yours, but you are not awake
and I must hold you faster now.

5 . SIDE OF THE ANGELS

The weak ones have gone now, thank God.
They crossed a line: too much time
in pavement cafes sighing at the city,
too much cognac on the job,
too much concern to blend in,
to get the fall of a jacket right, a fedora's tilt.

Our new guardians, you dare not meet their eyes.
Their gaze is way beyond compassion,
beyond good and evil, raw instinct.
No more urbanity. These are pure beast,
down on all fours again, because to make like men
was their undoing.

At last, says an old soldier, flicking ash
into an empty purse, *we have the angels we need,
not the ones we deserve.* He likens them to horses,
never fully broken, so when a bullet
kills the rider, who falls onto its neck,
a horse will never stop, but rather run

through squares and palaces,
oblivious until it folds, shattered, in a street
on the opposite side of the city,
and everyone can see its wild heart pounding,
like a man trying to get out, a new rider
trying to beat his way into the world.

6. MADONNA OF THE GAULOISES

I liked his style so much I took a risk.
That page where abyss stares into abyss
in my ill-thumbed paperback of Nietzsche's work
was where he left the matchbook.

I handed in my notice, found the Bar Pigalle,
took a corner table, back against the wall,
and waited. He was late, so late. Then later.
Curfew up, lights down. I placed an order.

My waiter warned to leave for my own good.
I long to know what's good for me, I said.
I felt no sense of purpose, still less
when the messenger turned up. No trumpets, no apologies,

he simply lit a *Caporal* and smiled
I've come to tell what I've been told,
but first I must be sure which side you're on.
In times like these it's hard to know . . . I straight up told him

no one could call me collaborator,
so he named some names and said a prayer.
He drank my noisette, claiming poverty,
took another cigarette and held it out to me.

I came to ask a favour – I began to
shake my head – *we hoped that you*
might carry something for us.
Then he put his finger on my lips and placed

that unlit filterless between them,
flicked a lighter, held the flame
in front of me. *No words,* he shook
his head, *but if it's 'yes', lean in and smoke.*

Spine fused, my tongue tied,
I feared this deal would leave me occupied,
invaded, and if so, what that might mean.
Sirens cried across the city, not to warn,

but more out of a sense of pity,
birds with empty nests. I thought, is he
for real? Can I answer with a codicil?
Why put the matchbook in *Beyond Good and Evil*?

No answers. He just stared. The flame grew shorter.
There were soldiers hammering at the door,
the waiter swore, tore off his apron,
ran for his life out through the kitchen.

7. THE ALL POWERFUL WORD

Is it any wonder, in the moments after,
that my mind's eye runs a rapid, flickering show
of flash-frames, faces, landscapes, lines I half-believe
from books, prayers, ads, an archipelago
of mad asymmetries?

After all, you set my skin alight. We steep in
it — that electricity — for all we're worth alive,
and the magic lantern settles on a single scene:
a tropical lagoon right here a million years ago,
before *here* meant a room in a city:

silence in the form of rain on leaves,
riffle of breeze in branches, and a lyre-bird —
no, a blackbird or a thrush — receives a gift,
a pearl in the throat, first note ever sung or heard,
the world's first elegy.

8. THE EXCHANGE or TAKES FOR THE MOMENT WHEN DIVINE BECOMES HUMAN, HUMAN DIVINE

(i)

Dining in a vast sky-blown hotel,
ex-lovers quail as one reaches out across the table
to meet the other's shaking hand.

(ii)

Hard winter, bridge over frozen river,
soldiers watch from checkpoints as one trench-coated
figure meets another, drops a briefcase.

(iii)

Miles from land, above the Southern Ocean,
a lone Antarctic petrel plummets.
Its beak breaks surface as the frame cuts.

(iv)

The universe flies apart, disrupts constellations
so instead of pictograms the heavens are a new
piano-roll we lack the technology to play.

(v)

Three armed police inspect the posts and ropes
of execution yards. In wide they look
like bridegrooms and the posts their brides.

It is time to tell the truth about stars.
They have no regard, no capacity for it,
can no more gaze upon the son of God

than walk into a room and place
a cool hand on his mother's skin, divine
him from a heel-jab on the other side.

Yet it is hard, as she lies sleepless,
listless on this summer night,
not to construe the stars' dead

un-pupilled eyes as witnesses,
especially that star – nameless, low,
not bright but somehow concentrated.

That one star, let's call it *Tendresse,*
could out-gaze each rooftop searchlight,
every arc of gunfire. Let it not be said

that *Tendresse* knows one mother,
one baby, one window from the next.
It is a raw vestigial need or pull

as when a wildcat makes a kill
because it sees a flash of rust-red tail,
not knowing the word *nightingale.*

10. FIRST COMMUNION OF
THE MADONNA

It is a closed set, for privacy:
a one-room apartment in some shabby *faubourg*,

single cameo light gives us a hunter's moon
through the cracked window.

Three months gone, she gazes out and in.
This scene demands rare intimacy.

It is a closed set in geometry too,
since it contains all its own boundaries.

O interloper, o squatter, o kicker,
o heel-jabber, scrapper, o thief-in-the-night,

o occupying power, you seized me,
now loose me, my lacrimae, my alchemy . . .

And as she speaks her lines we hear bootsteps
all over the city, as snipers, apparatchiks,

quislings, bankrupt officials, hit-men and hoods,
walk out with their hands in the air.

If this is a fracture across time and place,
where past and future hold each other's gaze,

then should the world not call a moment's halt,
not hang like a fly-cloud at head-height

when a downpour ends? Should it not let
fireworks burst, then hold their sculpted light?

Then we will see the glory of this wild,
this liberated city, where everyone is held

in green, red, gold of roman-candle arcs
and rocket seed-heads. We walk

among the rescued in their newly crowded bars.
A couple caught mid-kiss across

their table, waiter balanced on one foot
with eyes of steel and arms of plates.

A self-appointed prophet in a shirt and tie
gapes, fish-like, caught halfway through a lie.

I could lean and wet my fingertip
in stilled champagne, tilted on a singer's lip.

You could grab a smoke-ring from the ether
between punters and the pole-dancer,

pocket it as proof, then we could take the air
beside the float-glass river,

where a busker rests her bow on a string,
and you ask *what are all these flesh-ghosts thinking*?

Far from a cheap trick, this city-wide hiatus,
every held second comes at a cost.

We barely linger in this midnight space
before words rush back, before kiss meets kiss.

12. SOUND OF THE SON
BECOMING THE SON

Who put the lyre-birds on a loop?
The foley artist stays locked in all night
with shelves of vinyl, shellac, props,
but cannot conjure this.

She goes back to first principles,
how to sound the moment when eternal
word is spoken into flesh, tries temple bells,
thaw-drips, swish of samurai sword.

She runs the clip again and again:
a desert jackal lifts its head up into frame,
muzzle wet and red, and catches . . .
a chord, a cry, lip-smack, wave-crash,

some perfect sound that says:
all that ever was, and is, now gathers into this.
But then she hears an actor whisper
to a sleeping baby who will play her son.

She asks them to retake,
but by the time she puts a red light on
the child has woken hungry.
She concedes this scene to silence:

no sirocco, no sandstorm, no howl,
just the projector's endless hum and shuttle,
a sand-dog's blood-stained chops,
his dead eyes, his cocked ear.

Because the fire falters in the grate
since we prepared for winter far too late,

because the mistletoe has seized the oak,
and woodlands shiver nightlong in their soak,

because the ladder leans against your tree,
so they can climb and cut you down for me,

because the earth refused to split in two
in honour of the unearned gift of you,

because your love was misplaced in our hands,
and we will send you back with contraband,

because the air rushed in to light your lungs
and gave you endless love-and-colic songs,

because you have a date with us to keep,
a world that lies awake for you, *now sleep*.

14. MASSACRE OF THE INNOCENTS

It was just a handful – five or six –
but they spread themselves around us,
hid behind trees, began a *sotto voce*
incantation made of nonsense:
jingoistic rhymes, unsolvable riddles,
misplaced bits of liturgy.

But rattling as it did off countless boughs
and branches, this whispered cacophony
convinced us that an army
choked the forest. We pictured cities
laid to ruin on the roads from here,
battalions of starving, shattered men.

So we dropped our picks and knives,
knelt down, begged them to spare us.
As they trussed us up, one of them said
his had been a lullaby, then put his lips
up to my ear and sang:
lu lay, lu lay, o little tiny child . . .

If trees could walk like men,
beautiful boy-god, I would bear you
on my shoulders through this city,
show you every boulevard and alley,
every market stall and park.

You would tower above
the cavalcades and rallies,
peer into penthouse suites and boardrooms,
witness to so many acts of cruelty and love,
safe among my needles.

Then when you nod tired
in the cold and thickening dark
I would stand on the riverbank,
as long slow barges mutter by,
and sing you to sleep in my many tongues:

the bat-high silvered songs
of linden, plane; slow lullabies
of quince and medlar from the gardens;
long laments of empress, foxglove
in the windless squares.

I would carry you for years,
until you grow so heavy that they
nail you up to keep you here. It is needless,
because even if my back broke,
I would never let you fall.

I had the shape of a fall for days:
the slip, the heady rush, slow-motion vertigo,
unclear in details about where and why.

And then it came, on the Pantheon steps.
I lost my footing on the ice, and stone
caved under me, I fell and fell, kept

falling – Alice-like – until
down became my *still*, and all I knew of colours
was a vivid stream, a *trompe-l'oeil*

of sunset, or the end of the world.
After a while I found myself no longer steeled
against the crash, the foot of it all,

I lost belief that I would ever land,
and when I did, it felt as gentle as a coming
to attention. I raised my eyes to find

my body prone on floorboards
in an attic room. A director stepped over me,
fine-tuning lights to pick out this:

One actor with another in her arms.
Pietà. I had seen it before. She looked broken,
he more broken still, a map of cuts and burns.

The make-up was remarkable.
She gazed at him with unconvincing grief.
This take went on and on. Uncomfortable,

I stood up to look for flaws:
a pulse, a muscle-flick, but nothing stirred.
He had all the pull, the gravity of a corpse.

Is he alright? I said aloud,
and in a minute I was gone, thrown down
the stairs and out onto a busy road.

I turned up my collar with a shiver,
though it was not cold, looked left then right,
stepped out as if none of this was ever.

Day by day it thickens, as more pass on,
so we may find ourselves aware soon
of a cloud of witnesses, close around us,

walking in our steps behind,
each side of us, ahead, a sort of pressure,
but a good force, keeps us up and walking.

They still have names, not just *all souls*.
Although their names are never used
and they may struggle to recall them now.

The city streets are slower to negotiate,
now the heavenly host crowds in,
fleet and flicker in the corners of your eyes.

As their numbers quicken they get bolder,
and we sometimes catch one head on,
watching us with pity and agonising beauty.

Yours are so busy witnessing you
they barely notice, as you pass, the beggar's dog
which mouths a silent warning bark,

or the window-dresser lifting
dummies into place to form a wedding scene,
or the poplar trees, limbering up for a walk.

They miss the boy in a stolen bread van,
who weaves across the road to prove
that he is truly steering,

and the street-sweepers
with sticks and hand-carts full of spent fares,
all these with their own attendant clouds.

None of this sinks in, because their job
is just to witness you, not check up on
the coins you give to barmen, or street-sleepers,

nor which passers-by give you a smile,
but the subtleties of trust:
Do you live by grace? That is their only question,

as if they did when they were here,
as if they blazed through life in a perfect arc,
as if they drew a line between grace and luck.

Man of sorrows on a stick-back chair,
naked from the waist up, make-up wounded.
Around him a circle of track.

The camera completes another slow loop.
Reset. This shot could take all night,
until the circle is made perfect.

Outside, you can feel the pull,
resistance as the universe coils tight
around this attic room,

tows land-masses and tides behind it,
so a table slides towards a wall,
a car drifts in towards the curb.

And at the heart of it all, him,
past caring about retakes, thorn-crowned,
blind to the lens and gazing at us.

Anachronistic siren in the distance. Break.
We stretch our legs, but he stays put,
blood and tears still coming strong.

He is too good, his method too extreme,
we start to wonder if he cut himself for real
to get the colour right, to make it count.

19. GAZE OF TIME

I trust the calibration less,
now I've signed up for endlessness:
the street-sounds lift a semi-tone,
a disappointed waiter moans
about a tip, I catch his words
as chittering of moth-sized birds.
In smoky bars the dancers sweat
a touch more every night, and yet
if each day quickens on the last,
a broken clock that runs too fast,
then how to gauge how much we lose?
Extra wear and tear on shoes,
strain on larynx, books unread,
and somewhere on an ocean bed,
or scratched across the polar ice,
or scorched into a desert's face,
a wound left when eternity
broke into time to cut us free.

20. SEVEN DENOUEMENTS

(i)

Back from the lost, the one you miss the most
is at the door: *I've given up the ghost.*

(ii)

Old bells croak into voice to mark the hour,
a carillon of doves breaks from the tower.

(iii)

Gutters, grids and downpipes overflow.
You stand and soak, forgetting all you know.

(iv)

That song so sure you hardly dare begin –
you sing it, and an orchestra joins in.

(v)

A coin-toss: to set out again, or stay?
You snatch it from the air and walk away.

(vi)

All those feints, false trails, cross-purposes.
At last you catch yourselves off-guard and kiss.

(vii)

A blade cuts through the ropes – you are undone,
you kick the chair across the room and run.

III

FIREFLIES

I have stayed up far too late,
content to be mesmerised
as drab bugs are transfigured
by the open back-door's glow.
Gaudy, pinprick sparks,
they punch the fly-mesh screen
over and over, hard-wired
to reach their mother moon —
my naked hallway bulb.
And the real one hangs
impassive up beyond us all,
compelled by its laws
to keep tides on schedule,
to lend its pale gaze to
acts of passion and barbarism
with an equal blankness,
now blurred by the gauze
into a softer accent light,
almost compassionate.
Acceptance of necessity
is not enough to set me free.
For that, I have to love it.
I have stood here far too long.

I SAW ETERNITY THE OTHER NIGHT

As dusk outside began to steep,
I sat and waited for the shapes

of rooftops, geese, mill chimneys,
to soften as my window

pulled the world outside to in.
Self-portrait in a dim-lit room,

the street outside turned mirror
and my eyes reflected back as clear,

as simple, guileless as a dog's gaze.
Distemperate, I will not rise

tonight to my TV's illumined bait,
since all its shows, to captivate,

are cut and scripted with a sleight
to draw me in, then to spring shut.

Sleep now, replace this maudlin scene,
with one vast flawless empty screen

of screen in screen in screen in screen.

THE FACE IS THE SOUL OF THE BODY

Maybe it's a glitch in a game
and I'm just someone's avatar.
Except this barman's clearly analogue,
as is the cash I watched him counting out
as tonight's last drinker left.

I rest a sawn-off on his stubborn tongue
and wish I'd chosen vampire, Elvis,
not this rubber horse-head mask,
which reeks like a sweat-trap,
tightens on my throat.

I try to break the stand-off,
but new strong scents are drifting in,
musk follows grass, now soil and stone.
I'm trying to keep the heat on him,
but all the walls are closing in,

and I'm aching for a mercury drop
from my neck, for my spine to cantilever out,
for hands to cluster into hooves,
to be grazing in a field in rain,
in a cloud of my own steam.

YOUR DEFENCE TEAM

is reversing, fast, out of a space at the hypermarket
where they had to buy three months' supply of coffee
(can't get it by the jar) and this last straw has sparked
a rage in them at the catastrophe

of fates conspired to make this job – to win
your freedom back for you – so tough. First blow, forensics
nailed you to the spot; second, sifting through bins
the police found magazines with arrow slits

that matched the scrapbook note you sent
demanding cash with *non-sequential numbers,*
unmarked bills, no word to anyone, a drop-off point,
a distant, unmarked track. What master-plan of blunders,

drawn up from old movies on forgotten cable channels,
made you think that a cacophony of typefaces
would scramble all attempts to trace you? Meanwhile,
your hostage jumped free with tied-together laces.

Defence teams need caffeine for such a thankless task,
but not to shell out for a catering pack
and now their car's reversing camera broadcasts to the dash
a close-up of a blue-black blowfly racked

and writhing on a spider's web full-stretch across
the lens, so as they floor it backwards they watch
this magnified fight against captivity (an irony not lost
on them), as in that instant they look up to catch

their own eyes in the mirror, steel opaque,
not giving any ground. Poor fly winds itself dead centre
of the cobweb where all threads lead, until a truck
parked underneath a cherry tree (hair-netted to ensure

no birds can nest) jumps up to meet the camera,
and your defence team – trained to weigh the scale of harm –
can see the web is torn and no sign of its prisoner,
just an incandescent trucker, a sympathy of car alarms

and a host of witless bluebottles in bouffant trees
flaunting their careless, priceless, blousy liberty.

CLOUD OF UNKNOWING

The turtle's voice, joy without fear
Henry Vaughan

A guttering storm-shower.
A slide with its nose in a blow-up pool.
A radio adrift off its tinny jabber.
We drift in and out of heat haze,
unable to remember whose turn it is
to keep watch.

No song on this midsummer afternoon
but an atrial flutter
at the edge of our attention.

A flip-clock slaps through the minutes,
not breakneck but relentless.
Except we don't own such a clock
(couldn't sleep with it)

so it's a card-sharp working bars,
who false-cuts a pack
to keep the ace of hearts on top.
Only, in truth, it's more
a riffle than a cut
and comes in flurries,

so it's a departure-lounge Solari board,
that shuffles names of distant cities
in some destination raffle,

or, incarcerated in the past,
extravagantly vamped atlas moths
like pop-up books
squander their scant reserves
by folding and unfolding giant wings,

or more singular,
some long-abandoned prisoner
who shakes open
(held in quaking hand)
a tightly folded letter, reads in silence:
you have come to my attention . . .

but that catch in a paper trap
is a woodpigeon high in the crown
of a park-side tree,
in a thunderhead of leaves and ash-keys,

it stops then re-gathers for another burst,
chooses to be kept here,
captive to its own desire to be
crazed by the cross-hatch of branches,
to become undone.

CUSTODY OF THE EYES

After months of chin-on-chest,
shoes scuffed on frozen hillside tracks,
day-lit window dulled to lantern glow,
papered frame-to-frame with pages
from penitential psalms,
horizons contracted to the height of a man,

how do you choose
the moment to uncrick your neck,
to lift your head's dead weight,
you now unguarded, raw again and open to it all,
to take the sudden world in whole,
and hope your heart will hold?

And what if you squander it,
look up a second too soon,
attention and intention stolen by a dog's name
shouted in the valley below,
a branch brought down by its dry age,
your heart's own stammer.

PAID

On my journey into liberty
the trains were covered in graffiti.

They stopped at every halt
to let the ghosts get on and off.

In the city I was free.
I sold life insurance door-to-door,

married, had triplets, grandchildren.
The sea wore pebbles finer,

smaller every decade
– citrine, chert, carnelian, dolerite.

For many centuries the sun
played statues with me,

closing in, until each time
I turned it was a step or two nearer,

a shade more to the burn,
so I quickened my act, whipped

round faster and faster,
until one cloudless day I clocked it

mid-move and it had to go back
to start the whole thing over.

YOU ARE FREE TO GO

Us, the sullen, the unshackled,
lost without captivity,
a wide-berth shambles,
too tired to pass the time of day,

the ones who work the angles
and channels and cuts
with pockets full of rusted nails,
trying to trace a route by heart.

Or the *sotto voce* hitch-hiker who stops
you on a slip-road with a sign marked *NORTH*,
one hand folds the other in his lap,
a rough stone in his mouth,

a borrowed baseball cap tipped low –
because sun has never looked this strong –
with no idea how far to go.
Or this one, huddled on the last train,

curled up in a parka, sound asleep,
who sips at flat snakebite,
who reads the platform sign at every stop
without ever stepping out.

Or those who walk to wire-hedged cliffs,
backpacks chiming with old coins,
who trust the birds' instinctual paths,
and fly with seagulls, petrels, terns.

Now our mind-maps run
to pastel. Too many nights out soaked
in ditches, doorways, or hunched
in taprooms rehearsing plans and hopes.

We won't give up. We've come too far.
If that means stolen coats,
thumbed silent lifts, begged fares,
then so be it. So be it.

ON THE COMFORT OF SEEING YOUR OWN SHADOW AS THAT MEANS YOU ARE NOT LYING IN IT

Once I was granted my glorious liberty,
you might think I'd be set for life,

that I would sell the dog,
paint blue flames down the wagon's flanks,

mince all my credit cards,
quit eating till my fingers can't keep rings,

stuff cash into my boots,
stay out of banks and doctors' surgeries.

Instead, where once was me,
there's some quaking stranger holed up

in a rented room above a betting shop,
whose idea of liberty from fear

is being held tight all night by whoever,
to soothe the spirit via the body,

afraid of absolutely everything,
visible and invisible, trying to lose himself

in rainfall's interference patterns,
he mutters old petitions by rote,

the ones designed to armour you,
that he is told will operate like amulets

and every time his concentration drifts
he has to go back to the first line since

he is sure they only work if you mean them.
Saying them can never be enough.

FROM AN OPEN FIELD

Some days it is not a piece of land,
but field as in a box on screen,
or place in which a force prevails.

Start with this hawthorn tree
which marks where field meets ditch,
fly-tipped and litter-garlanded,

then zoom out to allotments,
a half-tended garden of earthly delights,
where a feral parakeet

seduces its reflection
in the glass of a long-scrapped,
half-rotted shed

until night drops and the other,
its perfect lover, its complementary half
is swallowed by the darkening frame

and the cock laments all night
until by sun-up its lack has drawn
all the greens out of the hills

the mosses and pitches,
all the billboards selling getaways,
and left the drained world pallid,

the parakeet itself lurid, furious and lime,
all the force of Spring used up
on one dance of misdirection.

ATTEMPTS AT A PORTRAIT

of a *doge* in a Venetian chair, but he is
running late — attending to affairs of state,
the winter swell of sad lagoons — and does not show.

Or of a *dog*, a liver-brown Dalmatian, who loves this
high chair when forbidden, but post-carnival,
when unclean streets are calling, will not sit.

Or of a *god*, too disconsolate to incarnate again,
who blessed the chair with fruit instead
by way of an apology, and yet cannot explain.

Or self-portrait as sitter, *gone*, as if he took
the last train out of town and in his wake
they felled the signals, locked all waiting rooms,

jemmied up the tracks, sent sleepers for sawdust
on floors of pigeon lofts and chicken coops.
Ozone is good for you, as is muzak from the bars

along the esplanade which complicates the air
like vespers, drowsy trees in evening's reddening,
a shadow falling through an empty chair.

COLLECT FOR THE DAY

Cold has come down
and with it, a shiver in the grass.

Things that today left behind
are being gathered in:

blossom, cats, yard-brushes, fish,
ripe bins, newspaper stands,

now office blocks —
pane by pane — now cars, cables,

radio waves, sunlight, highways,
all carried into our homes.

It is not easy to sleep
when there are oceans, savannahs

downstairs, but outside
the world is absolutely clear,

endless surface for the winds
to practise their angles,

for anyone who dares to step out
to dance their wildest,

a borderless night-long extravagance
that leaves them on

the other side of the world,
no landmarks, no maps,

but dawn will wait for them
to find their way back,

to open the door,
which opens all the doors.

IV
TAKK

God and all angels sing the world to sleep
Wallace Stevens

For what it's worth, a scatter-plot of misdirections:
distractions, inducements to look
in the wrong place, contents of days,
records, tilts, mirrors, misremembered lines from ads,
memorised street-maps with crucial errors,
trees where the road-signs should be,
ginnels with the names of boulevards,
trapdoors, slipcases, what must or cannot be said,
malcontents, masks, imagined distant shores.
And all along, it's open, obvious –
this wild, this ever-patient hope.

Something to wake up for, to talk about,
under the lindens, under sharp limes
that line this conduit, this corridor,
this urban pop-up artisanal caffeine-stop
fashioned out of land-locked shipping crates,
(faded cargo-line logos, authentic,
pixelated by Southern Ocean winds)
now host to Nordic-shanty-chic.
Its very name thanks you for your custom.
Every bean is single origin,
hand-picked for its freight of reek and shudder,
fridge-shipped all the way here from a farm
in the volcanic foothills of El Salvador.

The saviour of the world is here,
standing on one of the busiest tables,
in plain sight as if coaxed down from the sycamores,
his hands outstretched, wounds fruiting pear-drops
which fall at our feet like coffee drupes,
in cracks between the gritstone flags.
Maybe if he spoke up we would pass
the time of day, but he is semi-naked
and no one wants to look at that.

Strings of perma-festive lights in stripped poplars.
After dark they constellate at head-height,
but this morning they are cast as blank
by the spring blaze of it all.
You have to pinch them each to tell
if they are lit or not. Unseasonal,
a day before the hour goes on,
these dead strings, fake mistletoe,
apparition of an absence, ghost of ghost,
maker incognito inside made.

Sleep like you mean it, give it up for the ghost,
concede, become cargo and be carried forever.
It's hard to let this happen.
Sky is full, impossibly alive with joy,
or what appears to be.
Multi-tracked city on a mid-Lent night,
window-frames cracked for the first time this year,
terror of the future bittersweet as ever,
yet here is every consolation,
the present moment held as a stone
on your tongue, tastes like the ripe fruit
of a bourbon tree, the full-blooded
converse of rinsed-out, milksop mistletoe.

Scattergram of loosely-sketched-out rooks,
broken from an ash copse, wakes the dogs.
A heartbeat like a sucker punch.
Cranes bow over half-realised hotels,
watchful in their care.
Even in the darkness there are mirrors everywhere,
blind windows. Not to worry.
It is all about the outside here – signs of passion, love,
scanning faces in the hope of recognition.
A playlist of northern soul on loop.
Incarnadine beneath the skin.

What if the scene framed by this crate window
(off-white wall of office-block throws
spiny fruitless cherry tree into relief)
reveals itself in time as fog, not painted brick at all,
and then that fog reveals itself as smoke,
and somewhere out beyond the seat of fire
a vista well worth waiting for,
like some imagined *Finca Miravalle*
with swathes of ice-cream-bean and cypress trees
so vast, so over-burdened with held glory
that they nod and bow and spill.

Or what if the opposite: fog hardens to paint,
smoke sets as wall behind cherry boughs,
wall conceals a bare room on the other side
with windows facing out away from you,
sail-cloth curtains caught in breezes,
and a messenger who has been on the road for months –
filling up each night and driving through
the darkest hours solo, no hitch-hikers, no radio –
now pacing up and down not with impatience
but with nerves, preparing words for you –
rehearsing them out loud –
of welcome and you go or do not go.

Blossom like Absalom's hair, a catch of candyfloss,
his blaze and undoing in the riverside woods.
Semi-mature oaks, complete with galls,
trolleyed in, potted and spaced between the tables
in this makeshift rest-and-retail destination.
All in place they form a copse
and we believe in it. Above us roars
the Mancunian Way, but underneath its flyover
we live rainless and at liberty,
run for miles, hunt with impunity,
until oaks dwindle into bushes, scrub, grass, mud,
down into a reed-fenced, un-fished river,
where absolutely full looks like absolutely empty.

Reprieve. Relief. There will be more time.
Only the beginning to see here.
Frames of half-built Radisson Blus
charmed from their pits by crane-incantations,
creak-turns and ratchets.
Air-formed unmade bedrooms,
stage sets waiting to be acted-in,
containers for our vows, parties and redundancies.
Crane as trellis: creeper, rose, mile-a-minute vine
power up towards the source of daylight.

A photo-shoot of street food,
gloss-shots for next month's summer-menu launch.
False gods drop like blossom, gently as,
and all my own constructed faces of the maker fall away
revealing species of eyes I don't know how to read,
the real sustainer too innate,
too intimate, too untamed and immanent,
lost in the crowd and glad to take that risk.
This place a nod to Scandi-gratitude:
thank you, thank you . . .

Plane trees, scabbed and patched as dogs
with mange, self-flayed not
to become raw but to better flourish here,
to strip the mank and scuzz, to rise again,
naked but unflinched,
a chorus of full-leaf buttonwoods littering
the flagstones with their blank receipts.
Sometimes, when a pause breaks
the solid east–west belt of cars,
I am aware of a song,
but can't make out the words as yet.

NOTES & ACKNOWLEDGEMENTS

The phrase *lacrimae rerum* can be translated as 'the tears of things', as in the poem's title, and comes from Virgil's *Aeneid*. Its meaning is much disputed.

Skelmerdine Nurseries draws some of its details – including the story of Christmas-tree thefts – from a report in the *Macclesfield Express*.

My Window Becomes a Joseph Cornell Shadow Box refers to the glass-fronted display boxes created by the visionary American artist and film-maker. The phrase 'contracted to a span' comes from a hymn by Charles Wesley. The goldfinch, or *cardellino*, features in Renaissance painting as a symbol of the Passion, as in Raphael's *Madonna del Cardellino*.

Episodics is in memory of my father David.

The sequence **Vingt Regards** was written in response to Olivier Messiaen's set of twenty short piano pieces about the incarnation: *Vingt Regards sur l'Enfant-Jésus* (Twenty Contemplations of the Infant Jesus). Each piece has a subtitle, and each represents a particular *regard* upon the newborn Christ. For regard, read gaze or contemplation, but also a different angle on the scene. Some of the poems' titles nod to, or paraphrase, the music's subtitles. Messiaen began to write the piece in Paris under German occupation in 1944 and finished it in September after liberation. The fact that Marcel Carné was making possibly the greatest French film – *Les Enfants du Paradis* – in occupied Paris at the same time as Messiaen was writing *Vingt Regards* made the connection even more compelling.

Fireflies draws on some of Simone Weil's ideas in *On Science, Necessity and the Love of God.*

The Face is the Soul of the Body is a line from Ludwig Wittgenstein's *Culture and Value* (trans. Peter Winch, as is the epigraph on page 7).

Massacre of the Innocents draws on Messiaen's own account of his capture – with a small group of fellow musician-conscripts – by German soldiers in a forest near Verdun in June 1940, as related in *Olivier Messiaen: Texts, Contexts, and Intertexts (1937–1948)* by Richard D. E. Burton and Roger Nichols. The final line of the poem is a version of a line from the Coventry Carol.

At one stage of his Jesuit training, Gerard Manley Hopkins carried out the ascetic exercise known as **Custody of the Eyes**, in which he denied himself the sight of anything but the ground for weeks or months at a time.

Cloud of Unknowing takes its title from the anonymous Middle-English mystical text of the same name.

I Saw Eternity the Other Night is the first line of 'The World' by Henry Vaughan.

The Venetian Chair in **Attempts at a Portrait** was owned and painted by Henri Matisse.

Takk takes some of its geographical bearings from the café of the same name under the Mancunian Way in Manchester and from the El Salvadorian farms, notably Finca Miravalle, that supply its coffee beans.

I'm very grateful to the editors of publications in which these poems, some in earlier versions, appeared:

Arts Desk, BBC Radio 3, *Guardian*, *Irish Times*, *London Review of Books*, *Odes for John Keats* anthology (Keats–Shelley Memorial Association), *Poetry* (Chicago), *Poetry Ireland Review*, *Poetry London*, *RA Magazine*, *RSL Peace Poetry* pamphlet, *Tablet*, *Twelve Poems of Christmas* anthology (Candlestick Press).

Thanks are also due to Jean Sprackland, Karen Solie, John McAuliffe, Martin Dubois, Anna Webber, Seren Adams and to my editor Robin Robertson.

I'm grateful to the pianist Cordelia Williams for putting me together with Messiaen's *Vingt Regards*, and to Andrew Moorhouse for putting me together with the painter Jake Attree and publishing *Takk* as one of his Fine Press chapbooks.

And my thanks especially, as ever, to Ruth, Joe, Paddy and Griff.